Demi's Secret Garden

Poems compiled and illustrated by Demi

All are but parts of one stupendous whole,
Whose body Nature is, and God the Soul.

—Alexander Pope

Henry Holt and Company ◆ **New York**

The Grasshopper

The poetry of earth is never dead:
When all the birds are faint with the hot sun,
And hide in cooling trees, a voice will run
From hedge to hedge about the new-mown mead;
That is the Grasshopper's—he takes the lead
In summer luxury,—he has never done
With his delights; for when tired out with fun
He rests at ease beneath some pleasant weed.
The poetry of earth is ceasing never:
On a lone winter evening, when the frost
Has wrought a silence, from the stove there shrills
The Cricket's song, in warmth increasing ever,
And seems to one in drowsiness half lost,
The Grasshopper's among some grassy hills.

—John Keats

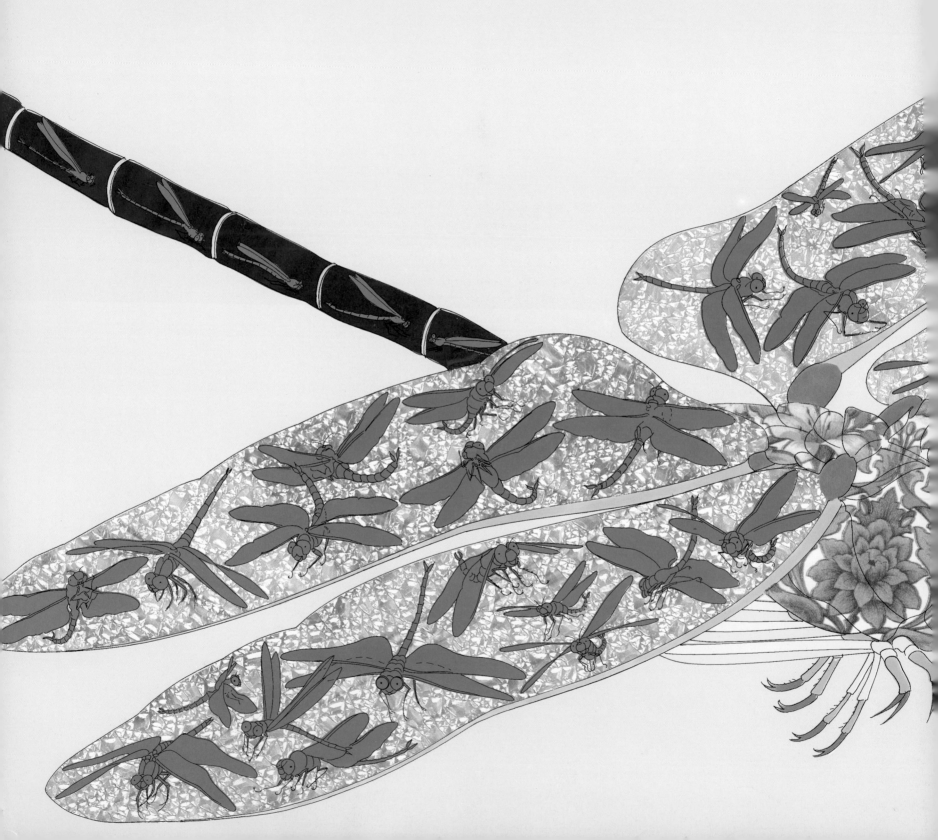

The Dragonfly

Dragonfly, dragonfly,
Sailing freely in the sky,
Gliding on the summer breeze,
Up and down as you please.
Flying alone, feeding in the sun,
Coming home when the day is done,
Free and happy in your heart,
Surely your life's a life apart.

—Chinese nursery rhyme

The Puss-Moth Caterpillar

The caterpillar that crawls through the mud
is covered in mud,
but transformed,
becomes the cicada that drinks dew
in the autumn wind.

—Hung Ying-ming

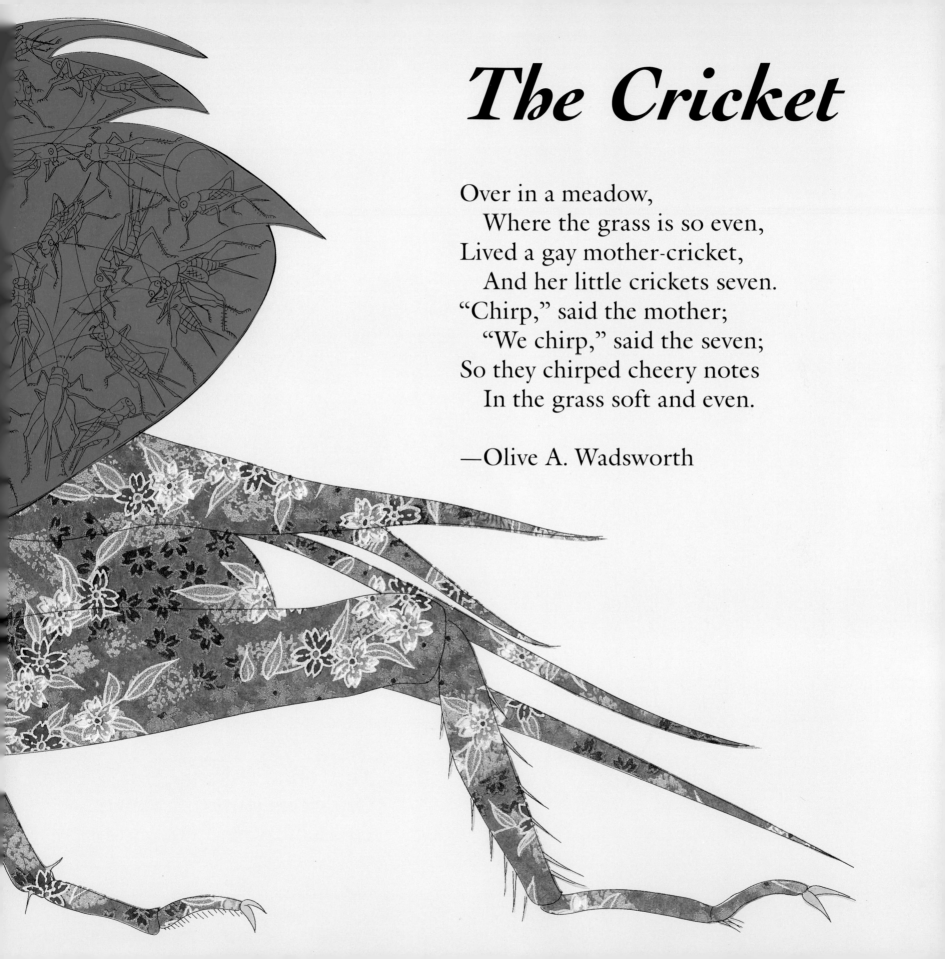

The Cricket

Over in a meadow,
    Where the grass is so even,
Lived a gay mother-cricket,
    And her little crickets seven.
"Chirp," said the mother;
    "We chirp," said the seven;
So they chirped cheery notes
    In the grass soft and even.

—Olive A. Wadsworth

The sound-color
Of insects pattering down
On the leaves.

—Chora

The Walking Leaf

The Daddy Longlegs

The body, born, is near its doom:
And riches are the source of gloom:
All meetings end in partings: yes,
The world is all one brittleness.

—*Panchatantra*

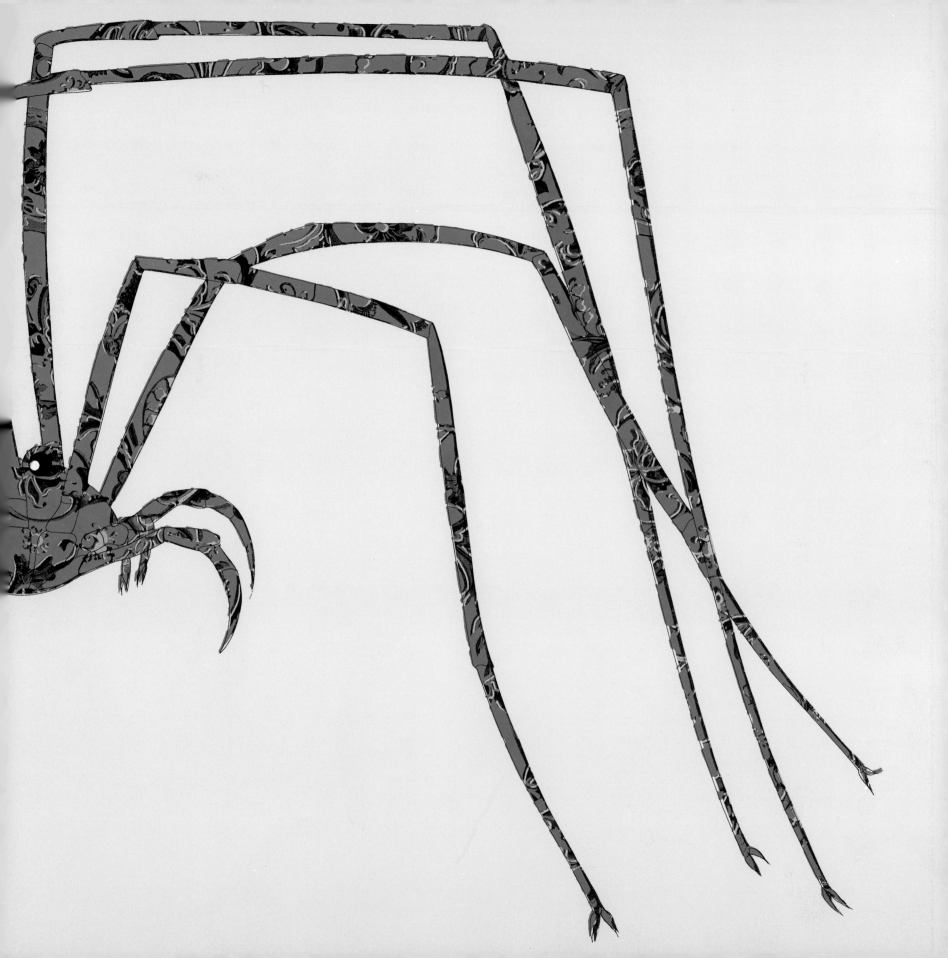

The Praying Mantis

The praying mantis
covets its prey
while the sparrow is flying at its back.
Within one contrivance there is yet another hidden.
Are wisdom and skill enough in life?

—Hung Ying-ming

The Mayfly

A mayfly—
Born to have just a glimpse
    Of the world.

—Anonymous, Japanese

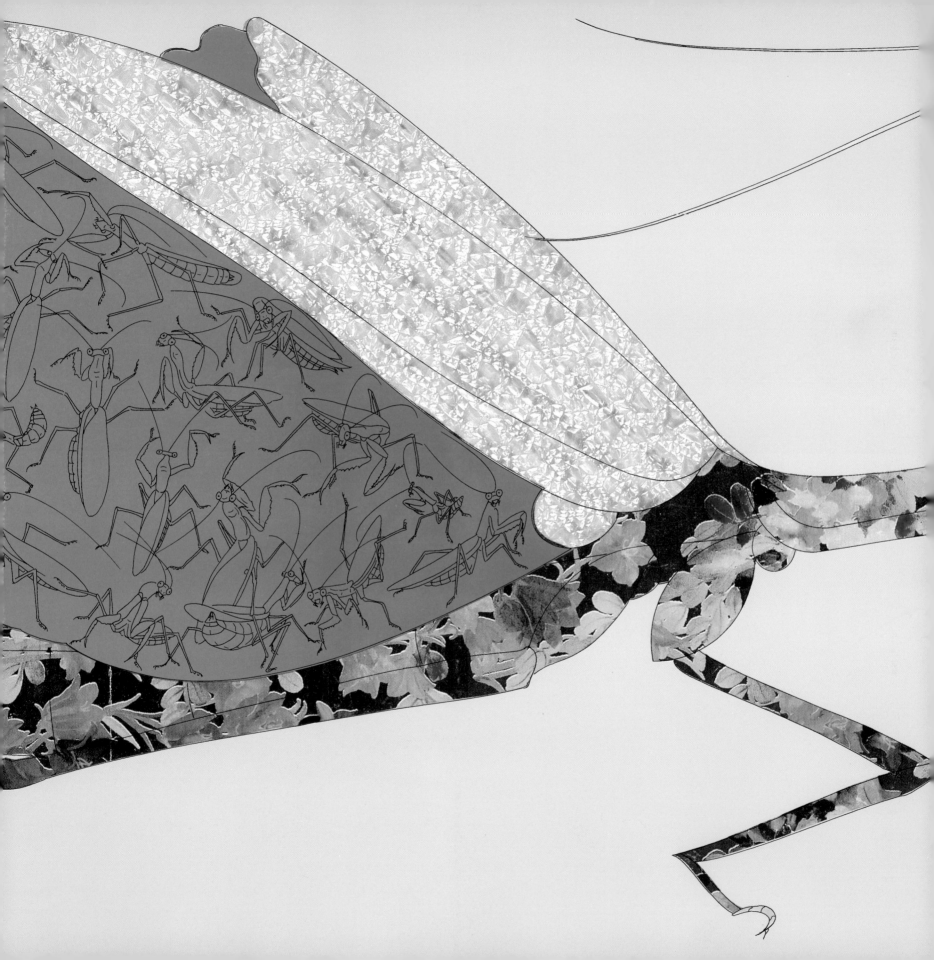

A noiseless patient spider,
I marked where on a little promontory it stood isolated,
Marked how to explore the vacant vast surrounding,
It launched forth filament, filament, filament, out of itself,
Ever unreeling them, ever tirelessly speeding them.

—Walt Whitman

The Spider

. . . So work the honey-bees,
Creatures that by a rule in nature teach
The act of order to a peopled kingdom.
They have a king, and officers of sorts,
Where some, like magistrates, correct at home;
Others, like merchants, venture trade abroad;
Others, like soldiers, armed in their stings,
Make boot upon the summer's velvet buds,
Which pillage they with merry march bring home
To the tent-royal of their emperor;
Who busied in his majesty surveys

The singing masons building roofs of gold,
The civil citizens kneading up the honey,
The poor mechanic porters crowding in
Their heavy burthens at his narrow gate,
The sad-ey'd justice, with his surly hum,
Delivering o'er to executors pale
The lazy yawning drone.

—William Shakespeare

The Bee

The Ant

Go to the ant, you sluggard,
watch her ways and get wisdom.
She has no overseer,
no governor or ruler;
but in summer she prepares her store of food
and lays in her supplies at harvest.

—Proverbs 6:6

The Housefly

Little Fly,
Thy summer's play
My thoughtless hand
has brush'd away.

Am not I
A fly like thee?
Or art not thou
A man like me?

For I dance
And drink, & sing;
Till some blind hand
Shall brush my wing.

If thought is life
And strength & breath,
And the want
Of thought is death;

Then am I
A happy fly,
If I live
Or if I die.

—William Blake

The Cicada

Discarded, one cicada's casket lay:
Did it utterly sing itself away?

—Bashō

The
Great Gray
Owlet Moth

The desire of the moth for the star,
  Of the night for the morrow,
The devotion to something afar
  From the sphere of our sorrow.

—Percy Bysshe Shelley

The Firefly

The rain tries to dim your light,
The wind makes it glow the more.
Why not fly to heaven afar,
And twinkle near the moon—a star?

—Li Po

Beetles

The Birdwing Butterfly

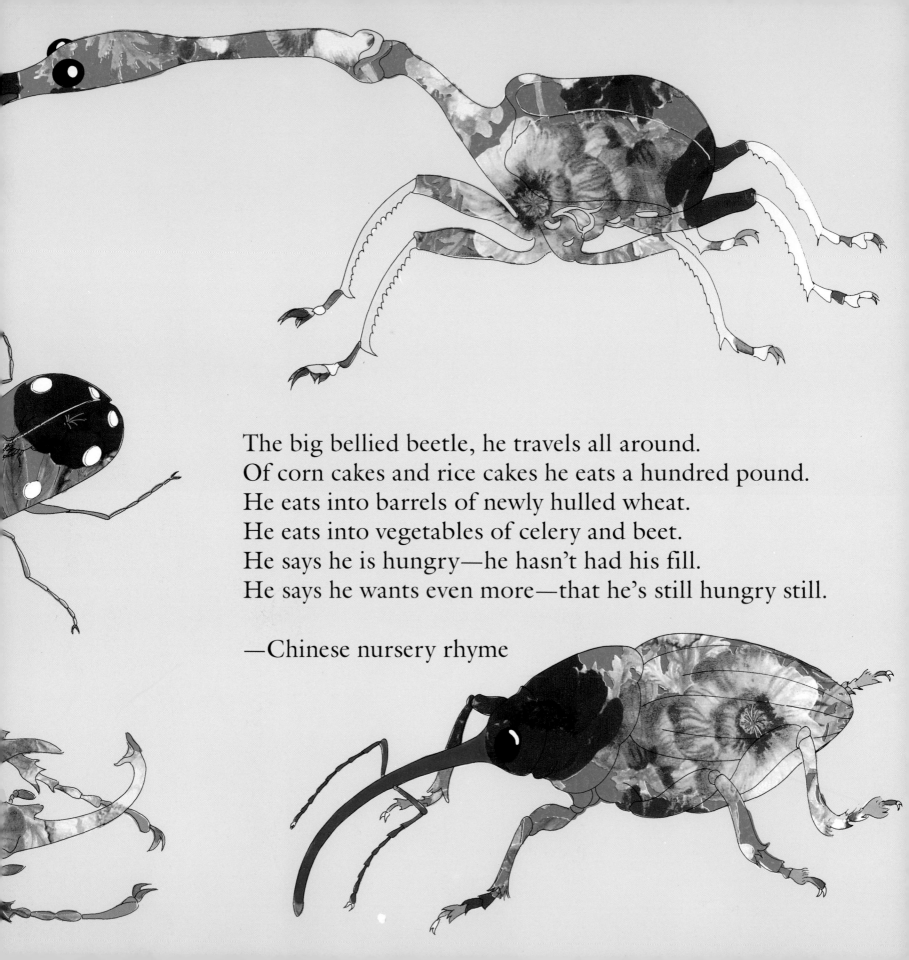

The big bellied beetle, he travels all around.
Of corn cakes and rice cakes he eats a hundred pound.
He eats into barrels of newly hulled wheat.
He eats into vegetables of celery and beet.
He says he is hungry—he hasn't had his fill.
He says he wants even more—that he's still hungry still.

—Chinese nursery rhyme

The Walkingstick

A walkingstick
On a plum-tree limb—
You catch me,
And I'll catch him!

—Chinese nursery rhyme

Brown and furry
Caterpillar in a hurry;
Take your walk
To the shady leaf, or stalk.

May no toad spy you,
May the little birds pass by you;
Spin and die,
To live again a butterfly.

—Christina G. Rossetti

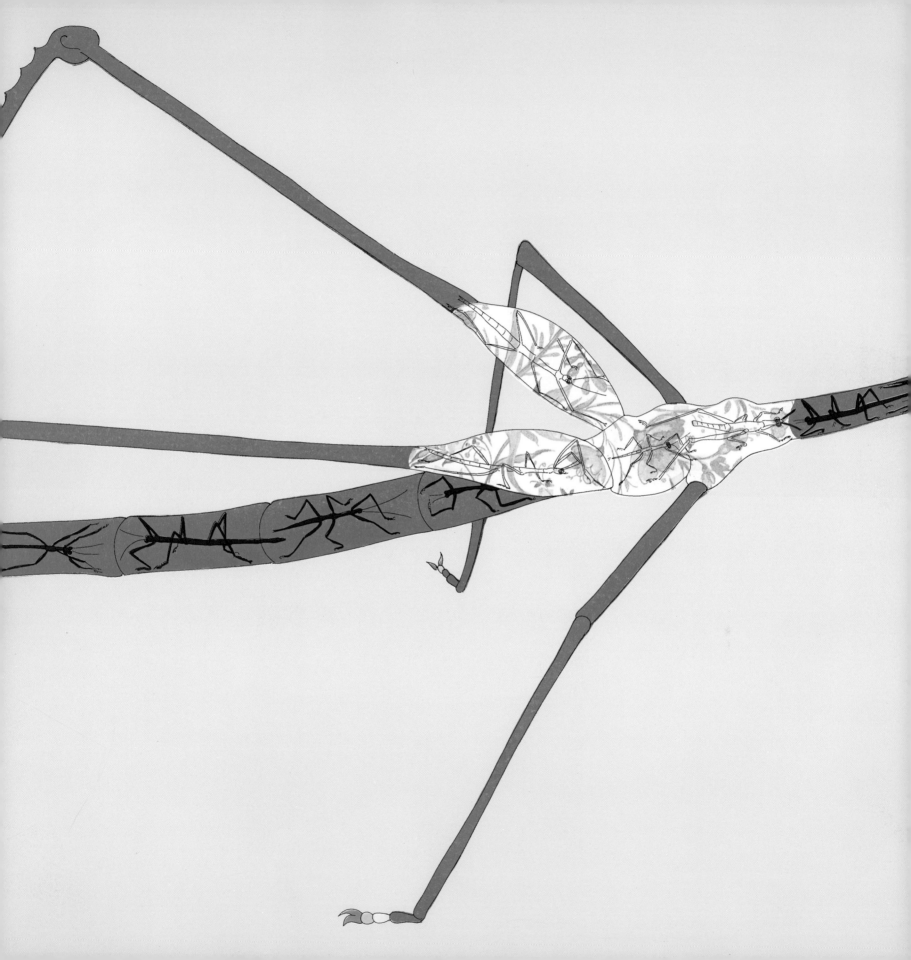

Afterword

Treehopper

The enlarged prothorax, or midsection, of the Treehopper bulges out over the head and tail of this most extravagant of insects. Though it can run, jump, and fly surprisingly well, most of the time the Treehopper crouches motionlessly, looking like a thorn, berry, or spike of wood.

Grasshopper

Grasshoppers are generally large insects. Some exceed four inches in length. They are super jumpers because of their greatly enlarged hindlegs. They like to eat nearly all plants both cultivated and wild, but in some parts of the world, people like to eat them—dried, jellied, roasted, and dipped in honey or ground into meal!

Dragonfly

This large, fearless insect is almost impossible to catch—too quick and alert! The Dragonfly captures its prey on the wing, flying low to the ground along well-established routes and perches. Some Dragonflies even hunt Honeybees, earning them the nickname Bee Hawk.

Puss-Moth Caterpillar

This extraordinary-looking caterpillar has a forked tail that ends in two rods. When threatened, the Puss-Moth Caterpillar flips the fork forward and sprays a sharp odor from the red tips, at the same time oozing a stinking liquid from below the head. Not a tasty meal!

Cricket

The male Cricket's loud chirping noise is made in much the same way as the Katydid's call. Crickets feed on seeds, leaves, and fruit. If one gets into your house, it may decide to take a bite out of your wool sweater.

Walking Leaf

Master of camouflage, the Walking Leaf is almost indistinguishable from the leaves around it. But if it is discovered, the Walking Leaf is far from defenseless—it can squirt a foul-smelling, burning liquid at its enemies.

Daddy Longlegs

An arachnid, not an insect, the Daddy Longlegs has unusually long, slender legs. It likes to hang upside down in dark, musty corners.

Mayfly

The Mayfly nymph, or immature stage, may live at the bottom of a stream for a year or more, but once it leaves the water, it doesn't have long to live. Within just a few days the Mayfly molts twice to become an adult, reproduces—and then dies.

Praying Mantis

Sitting motionless on a tree, the Mantis appears to be praying. But the peaceful posture belies a fierce temperament. If a butterfly or other insect comes along—watch out! The Praying Mantis seizes its victim with its powerful forelegs and quickly devours it.

Jumping Spider

Like the Daddy Longlegs, the Jumping Spider is not an insect—it's an arachnid, more closely related to scorpions and ticks than to cockroaches. The Jumping Spider hunts by pouncing upon its prey, often leaping many times its own length—but not without a safety rope. Before jumping, it secures a silk thread to clamber back up if it misses its mark.

Honeybee

When the day is hottest, the Honeybee begins its work. And each Honeybee has a specialized job. Drones attend the queen. Workers collect pollen and nectar from flowers and make the wax combs and honey. Honeybees can live in colonies of 20,000 or more, though each colony is ruled by a single queen.

Ant

The most numerous and widespread of all land animals, the Ant is remarkably long-lived—workers live up to seven years, and queens to fifteen. Most of the Ants you see are workers, which do not have wings; only fertile males and females fly. For its size, the Ant is extremely strong, capable of lifting objects many times its own weight.

Housefly

The stout, active, bristly Housefly will eat just about anything and can live just about everywhere. Though it doesn't bite, the Housefly can transmit diseases such as typhoid, dysentery, and cholera by touching food that is then eaten by humans.

Cicada

The male adult Cicada sings morning, noon, and night, thrumming a pair of drums on the sides of his abdomen, creating an uproar that can be heard over a quarter of a mile away. Southern Cicada nymphs live underground for thirteen years before emerging, while their northern cousins come out once every seventeen years.

Great Gray Owlet Moth

Found from the tropics to the polar regions, the Great Gray Owlet Moth feeds on flowers, fruits, and the juices of trees. It can detect the sounds of predatory bats and avoid them with dizzying flight maneuvers. The Great Gray Owlet Moth can also mimic their calls, jamming the bats' "sonar" long enough to escape.

Firefly

At twilight the slow-flying male Firefly appears and disappears in the distance as it flashes on and off, hoping to attract a mate. Though it doesn't fly, the female flashes too, as does the nymph—which is why they are also called Glowworms.

Beetles

There are over 300,000 different kinds of beetles, ranging from the nearly microscopic Red Spider Mite Destroyer to the Hercules Beetle, which can grow to be over seven inches long. Beetles have leathery forewings, called elytra, that meet in a straight line down the center of the back and serve as a protective covering. Most beetles feed on plants, and some are very destructive; but many beetles eat other insects, including many pests.

Birdwing Butterfly

The largest and most beautiful butterfly of Southeast Asia, the Birdwing Butterfly can grow up to eleven inches across—the size of a robin! Because Birdwing Butterflies usually congregate around the tops of jungle trees, they are difficult to catch and are highly prized by collectors.

Walkingstick

Like the Walking Leaf, the Walkingstick is a talented mimic. It lives in oak, black locust, or wild cherry trees, hiding by day and feeding on the leaves at night. The Walkingstick is quite large—growing over a foot long— and some people keep them as pets.

To see a World in a Grain of Sand
And a Heaven in a Wild Flower,
Hold Infinity in the palm of your hand
And Eternity in an hour.

—William Blake, "Auguries of Innocence"

Acknowledgments

Treehopper: From "An Essay on Man" by Alexander Pope, 1688–1744
Grasshopper: "On the Grasshopper and the Cricket" by John Keats, 1795–1821
Dragonfly: Chinese nursery rhyme adapted by Tze-si Huang from the translation
by Isaac Taylor Headland
Puss-Moth Caterpillar: Hung Ying-ming, sixteenth-century Chinese poet
Cricket: From "Over in the Meadow" (1871) by Olive A. Wadsworth
Walking Leaf: Chora, Japanese poet, 1729–81
Daddy Longlegs: From the *Panchatantra*, translated by Arthur W. Ryder
Mayfly: Unknown Japanese poet
Praying Mantis: Hung Ying-ming, sixteenth-century Chinese poet
Spider: From "A Noiseless Spider" by Walt Whitman, 1819–92
Honeybee: From *Henry V,* act I, scene ii, by William Shakespeare, 1564–1616
Ant: Proverbs 6:6
Housefly: "The Fly" by William Blake, 1757–1827
Cicada: Bashō, Japanese poet, 1644–94
Great Gray Owlet Moth: From "To——" by Percy Bysshe Shelley, 1792–1822
Firefly: Li Po, Chinese poet, A.D. 701–762
Beetles: Chinese nursery rhyme adapted by Tze-si Huang from the translation
by Isaac Taylor Headland
Birdwing Butterfly: "The Caterpillar" by Christina Georgina Rossetti, 1830–94
Walking Stick: Chinese nursery rhyme adapted by Tze-si Huang from the translation
by Isaac Taylor Headland

Library of Congress Cataloging-in-Publication Data
Demi/Demi's secret garden / by Demi.
Summary: Excerpts from Walt Whitman, the Bible, Chinese nursery rhymes, and other literary sources
accompany illustrations of such insects as the cricket, grasshopper, and puss-moth caterpillar.
ISBN 0-8050-2553-7
1. Insects—Literary collections. [1. Insects—Literary collections.] I. Title. II. Title: Secret garden.
PZ5.D38De 1993   808.81'936—dc20   92-27204

Printed in Hong Kong
1 3 5 7 9 10 8 6 4 2